UNLEASHING BRILLIANCE

A Roadmap to Confidence for Black Professionals

KK Harris – Business Coach Psychologist

This is a work of non-fiction.

Copyright © 2023 KK Harris

All reserved. No part of this book may be reproduced or used in any manner without written permission of the copyright owner except for the use of quotations in a book review. For more information, address: kk@kkharris.co.uk

First Kindle edition July 2023

Please follow me on my social media which includes my YouTube channel, Instagram and a link to this book.

When you follow let me know that you bought the book so I can personally thank you.

Kind regards,

KK Harris

FOREWORD

It is with great pleasure and heartfelt anticipation that I introduce this book to you – the dedicated, hardworking, yet possibly overlooked or undervalued professional. You are reading this because you yearn for more, because you believe in the magnitude of your potential, even if it seems shrouded in uncertainty at times. This book is the manifestation of that belief – a testament to your courage to step up and reclaim your confidence.

Throughout my years of experience as an executive coach, I have had the profound privilege of guiding hundreds of individuals on their journey to personal and professional empowerment. Among them, the most resonant stories have been those of Black professionals who, despite their extraordinary talents and potential, have faced unique challenges that have often left them questioning their worth and place in their careers.

But here's the thing, these challenges are not insurmountable. I've witnessed first-hand the awe-inspiring transformation that occurs when individuals awaken to their inherent power and channel it towards their professional pursuits. I've seen the impact it can have, not just on their careers but on their entire lives. Their stories, their triumphs, their journeys to unleashing their brilliance - these are the catalysts that inspired this book.

This is not just another self-help guide filled with empty promises. It is a toolbox – a collection of actionable strategies grounded in years of research, empirical evidence, and real-world application. But more importantly, it is a bridge, linking you to the confident, empowered professional you aspire to be.

This journey will require introspection, persistence, and courage. It will not always be comfortable, but growth rarely is. You'll be asked to examine the depths of your self-belief, question long-held assumptions, and dare to dream bigger than you ever have. But remember, you are not alone in this. I will be there with you, guiding you every step of the way.

Each chapter of this book brings you one step closer to understanding the magic within you, the power of your voice, and the immense potential that lies in networking, sponsorship, and intentional growth. And in the end, you'll realise that the confidence you seek is not elusive or external – it's been within you all along, waiting to be kindled.

As you turn these pages, I want you to hold on to this one truth: You are enough. You are worthy. And you have everything you need within you to reclaim your confidence and unleash your brilliance.

So, dear reader, embark on this journey with an open heart and mind. Your path to unparalleled professional growth and self-empowerment awaits.

Always in your corner,

KK Harris

ACKNOWLEDGEMENTS

Writing this book has been an emotional, intellectual, and transformative journey, a journey that would have been impossible to undertake without the steadfast support and inspiration of several incredible individuals in my life. Today, I want to take a moment to acknowledge them.

First and foremost, I want to express my deepest gratitude to my daughter, Ty. Her wisdom, far beyond her years, has consistently reminded me of the power of my voice and the impact it can have. She is my reminder to never shrink but rather to expand and let my words echo far beyond the confines of my home office. Ty, you are the legacy that I am building, the source of my pride and my unending motivation. I hope this book makes you as proud of me as I am of you.

To all the Black professionals I have had the distinct honour to coach over the years, this book would not exist without you. Your stories, your challenges, your victories, and your resilience have been my inspiration and my driving force. You are the reason I penned this journey towards empowerment and self-belief.

To my rock, my champion, Raymond, thank you for always standing by my side, pushing me to show up boldly, and reminding me of the power of courage. You understand that our work is not just about personal achievement; it's about affecting lives positively, and for that, I am ever grateful.

I also want to acknowledge two monumental figures who have profoundly shaped my understanding of justice, equality, and resistance: Angela Davis and James Baldwin. Angela's relentless fight for social justice, the rights of women, and the queer and transgender community is an inspiration like no other. Baldwin's impassioned call to "end the racial nightmare" continues to fuel my drive for equity and fairness. Both of them have guided me in my journey, pushing me to be the change I seek.

This book, thus, is a tribute to each one of you - your struggles, your strength, your courage, and your brilliance. As you read the words etched on these pages, know that they are, in essence, a testament to the power of our shared humanity and the unyielding spirit of progress.

With utmost gratitude and respect,

KK Harris

INTRODUCTION

Hello, reader. If you're holding this book, there's a good chance you're looking to reignite your inner fire and regain a sense of confidence that will fuel your professional journey. I want to assure you, you're in the right place.

If you find the insights and strategies in this book useful and want to further your journey of professional development, I invite you to follow my YouTube channel, KK's Career Advice.

There, I provide regular content focused on career advice and personal growth tailored specifically for Black professionals. From tackling day-to-day challenges at work to more strategic career planning advice, my videos are designed to offer continued support and guidance as you navigate your professional journey. Let's continue this journey of growth and success together. See you there.

As a Black Executive Coach and Business Psychologist, I've spent years working with individuals who, like you, are seeking to navigate the complex maze of their careers. Over this time, one thing has become abundantly clear: Black professionals, due to their minority status within organisations, are less likely to be offered professional coaching. Consequently, these individuals often struggle with a unique set of challenges that require tailored guidance and support.

This is why I've written this book – to provide the needed coaching and advice to those Black professionals seeking a helping hand. This book is the result of my personal experiences, observations, and expertise, all of which have allowed me to deeply understand and resonate with the lived experiences of Black professionals. It's a guide and a friend, inspired by my work, that seeks to give you the tools, strategies, and self-belief necessary to thrive in your career.

Across the pages that follow, we will walk together through a journey of self-discovery and growth, focusing on core aspects such as developing a growth mindset, enhancing your communication skills, and harnessing the power of networking and mentorship. We'll delve into the strategies that can help you secure a sponsor and the ways to chart your path forward.

But this is not just a book of tactics and strategies. At its core, this book is about restoring your confidence, particularly if you've dealt with any form of career trauma. We will explore how to rebuild this foundational trait through gratitude, intentional self-empowerment, and understanding how to leverage the power of your brain.

This book is a step towards bridging the gap in professional coaching for Black professionals. It is a testament to the fact that, as a Black professional, your voice matters, your experiences are valid, and your success is attainable. My sincere hope is that these pages inspire you, guide you, and, above all, empower you to unleash your brilliance.

Welcome to this journey. I'm thrilled and honoured to be your guide.

CONTENTS

Chapter 1

RECOGNIZING MICRO-AGGRESSIONS AND WORKPLACE BIAS

Welcome to Chapter 1, where we delve deep into the heart of our discussion: understanding the nuances of micro-aggressions and workplace bias. It's a sensitive topic, with roots reaching into the core of our identities, but it's also the starting point for transformative change. Let's shed light on these challenging issues to gain understanding, foster empathy, and, ultimately, reclaim our confidence.

Defining Micro-aggressions and Workplace Bias

Before we delve into the impact, let's take a step back to understand the terms. Though they may sound insignificant, micro-aggressions hold a disproportionate amount of power. These are everyday slights or indirect, unintentional discriminations that chip away at your sense of self and belonging. Seemingly harmless comments or actions may carry an undercurrent of racial prejudice or stereotype, leaving you feeling othered, diminished, or just plain exhausted.

Take the example of hair. Hair is a personal matter. Yet, as a Black woman in a professional setting, you may have found your afro hair to be an unwarranted point of curiosity. A colleague asking to touch your hair might seem like simple curiosity, but it reduces you to an object of novelty, an exhibit in a corporate zoo. This action subtly communicates that you are different and that you do not fully belong.

Workplace bias, while more overt, is an unfair prejudice based on protected characteristics such as race, gender, or age. This can manifest in many ways, from being overlooked for promotions to finding your ideas credited to someone else. The effects, while more obvious, are no less damaging.

Let's also touch on another common micro-aggression: the compliment that's not quite a compliment. Have you ever been told, "You're so articulate," or "You speak so well"? While these words might be packaged as praise, they carry a veiled insult, suggesting surprise that someone of your racial background can express themselves eloquently. These words perpetuate harmful stereotypes and subtly reinforce racial hierarchies. They undermine your achievements and make you question your worth.

The Impact on Performance and Mental Health

The cumulative effect of these micro-aggressions and biases can deteriorate your mental health and work performance. Each slight chips away at your confidence erodes your sense of worth and contributes to feelings of alienation and imposter syndrome.

One of the most damaging effects is the erosion of psychological safety — the feeling that you can be your authentic self without fear of negative consequences. In a psychologically safe environment, you can voice your thoughts in a meeting, express your feelings, and take creative risks. When micro-aggressions and biases compromise this safety, your mental health suffers and your performance dips. You become less likely to contribute to meetings, less likely to propose new ideas, and less likely to take on leadership roles.

Confronting Micro-aggressions with Courage and Grace

In the journey of navigating a workplace where you face micro-aggressions, one of the most empowering steps you can take is to confront the source.

This section is dedicated to helping you do just that, all while maintaining your dignity, poise, and professionalism. Remember, our aim isn't to fight fire with fire. Our goal is to spark enlightening conversations that sow the seeds of change.

The Power of Speaking Up

Micro-aggressions are often born out of ignorance, not malice. This doesn't make them any less harmful, but it does suggest a path to resolution. If someone is unconsciously perpetuating harmful stereotypes or biases, bringing this to their attention might be the wake-up call they need.

Let's be clear: speaking up isn't just about educating others; it's about self-preservation. Bottling up resentment and frustration doesn't lead to peace - it leads to distrust, deep-seated anger, and a stifling of your potential. You start pulling yourself back, shielding yourself from opportunities, all in a bid to protect your emotions. This isn't a path to growth, and it certainly isn't a path to happiness.

The Art of the Conversation

Now, how do you go about having these conversations? Start by assuming good intent. Give the person the benefit of the doubt. This doesn't mean excusing their behaviour. It simply means approaching the conversation from a place of seeking understanding rather than levelling accusations.

Choose a private setting to avoid unnecessary embarrassment and be direct but polite. Explain the incident, express how it made you feel, and kindly suggest an alternative way they could have acted or a change in behaviour for the future.

Seeking Support

Let's face it; confronting micro-aggressions can be a daunting task, especially if it involves speaking up to a superior. In such situations, don't hesitate to seek support. This could be a trusted colleague, a mentor, or even a member of the HR team. Having someone present can provide moral support and ensures there's a third-party witness who can attest to the proceedings of the conversation.

Also, remember that there are resources within your organisation designed to help you navigate these tricky waters. If your organisation has an HR department, they may provide conflict resolution or mediation services.

The Road Ahead

Confronting micro-aggressions is a significant step, but it's only a part of your journey. It won't miraculously end all biases or cure the workplace of all its problems overnight. However, it's a decisive step in reclaiming your peace, asserting your worth, and transforming your environment, one conversation at a time.

The road may be rocky, and the path might be steep, but you're not walking it alone. So, let's draw a deep breath, square our shoulders, and take that step forward, one brave stride at a time.

The Invisible Barrier - Navigating Systemic Obstacles

Since the heart-wrenching murder of George Floyd, the world has undergone a profound awakening. Companies worldwide have stepped up, acknowledging past mistakes and pledging to create more inclusive, nurturing spaces for Black talent. While change won't occur overnight, there's a discernible shift, and organisations are putting in the work to be better. However, these promises come too late for some. They've already moved on, their potential stunted by invisible, systemic barriers.

Understanding Systemic Barriers

Systemic barriers are not merely abstract concepts. They are flesh and blood, housed within the very structure of the organisations we work in. They are individuals entrenched in old ways of thinking, clinging to outdated biases, and perpetuating a culture that stymies progress.

When you experience systemic racism or discrimination, it's important to remember that it does not reflect your capabilities or worth. It's a manifestation of the deeply entrenched biases of individuals within the organisation. Their refusal to acknowledge and address these biases is what creates these systemic barriers.

Breaking Free from the Chains of Discrimination

The call to break free from the chains of discrimination can often be drowned out by the humdrum of daily work life. When caught in the throes of delivering projects, meeting deadlines, and attending meetings, it's easy to lose sight of the larger picture - your growth, your happiness, and your peace of mind.

Furthermore, the prospect of venturing into the unknown can be daunting. But remember, it's not an abyss you're stepping into; it's a realm of opportunities teeming with potential. Let's take a simple yet powerful tool, LinkedIn. On this platform, you can explore a wealth of job opportunities and network with professionals worldwide. Diving into the jobs section on

LinkedIn can help you gauge your worth in the career market. You can see the kinds of roles that your skills and experience qualify you for and the organisations that are actively seeking your expertise.

Taking Control - Crafting Your Way Forward

The first step to breaking free is to equip yourself with a powerful CV or resume. Highlight your skills, experiences, and achievements. Show potential employers what you bring to the table.

Seek professional advice from a business psychologist or a career coach. They can provide valuable insights and strategies to rebuild the confidence eroded by systemic barriers. They can guide you in identifying organisations that value diversity and offer you the growth opportunities you deserve.

Seek a Better Future

Now that you're equipped with a robust CV and renewed confidence, it's time to step into action. Don't be hasty in your search for a new work home. Use the power of the internet to make informed decisions. Websites like Glassdoor offer an insider's perspective into various organisations.

You can discover what current and past employees have to say about their experiences, the company culture, the opportunities for growth, and more. Pay particular attention to reviews by Black employees, as these will give you valuable insights into the company's inclusivity and diversity practices.

It's also worth exploring reviews of your current company. We often become so engrossed in our own experiences that we overlook the broader issues at play within the organisation. Reading other employees' experiences may reveal patterns and systemic issues you weren't aware of.

In the end, remember that you are not alone. There are organisations out there striving to do better, to be inclusive and supportive spaces for their diverse talent. It's about finding these organisations and seizing the opportunities they offer. Don't let the fear of the unknown hold you back. Armed with your skills, talents, and knowledge of your worth, you are ready to step into a future that values you and encourages you to reach your full potential.

To sum up, the internet is a powerful tool that can reveal the true face of an organisation. Make use of it to ensure that your next step is towards a future that respects and appreciates you. And always remember, you are not merely navigating systemic barriers; you are shattering them. You are not defined by the walls around you but by your ability to overcome them and forge ahead with courage, strength, and unshakeable determination.

Chapter 2

THE NARCISSISTIC LEADER - UNDERSTANDING AND NAVIGATING THEIR WEB

Spotting the Narcissist

Understanding Narcissism: To navigate the labyrinth of a narcissistic leader, we first need to comprehend the nuances of narcissism. Narcissism isn't simply about taking too many selfies or craving the spotlight. It is a complex personality disorder that can lead to harmful behaviours, especially in positions of power.

The Diagnostic and Statistical Manual of Mental Disorders, 5th Edition (DSM-5) defines Narcissistic Personality Disorder as a mental condition in which people have an inflated sense of their importance, a deep need for excessive attention and admiration, troubled relationships, and a lack of empathy for others. However, behind this mask of extreme confidence lies a fragile self-esteem that's vulnerable to the slightest criticism.

DSM-5 lists nine potential criteria for narcissistic personality disorder. Notably, to be diagnosed, an individual only needs to meet five out of these nine. The criteria include having a grandiose sense of self-importance, preoccupation with fantasies of unlimited success, power, brilliance, beauty, or ideal love, a belief that they're special and can only be understood by or associate with special people or institutions, needing excessive admiration, having a sense of entitlement, exploiting others for their gain, lacking empathy, being envious of others and believing others are envious of them, and showing arrogant, haughty behaviours or attitudes.

When such an individual is in a leadership role, their need for admiration, lack of empathy, and manipulation can create a toxic environment. Their refusal to accept criticism, combined with their tendency to belittle others to assert their superiority, can breed fear and stifles the team, and it often leaves the employees feeling undervalued and dismissed.

It's important to note that not every narcissist is a leader, and not every leader is a narcissist. However, the position of power that comes with leadership roles can be incredibly attractive to individuals with narcissistic tendencies, hence the higher prevalence in those positions.

In the subsequent sections, we will delve deeper into identifying narcissistic behaviours, dealing with narcissistic leaders, and strategies to maintain your confidence and sanity while working under them.

Identifying Narcissistic Behaviours

Cracking the Narcissistic Code: It's time to lift the veil and reveal the distinct traits that paint the portrait of a narcissistic leader. They're not always obvious, and it's easy to get ensnared by their charisma or the illusion of their 'perfection.' So, buckle up as we dive into the complex world of narcissistic behaviours.

First and foremost, narcissistic leaders are masters of charm. Their charisma can be as bright as a star, pulling everyone into their orbit. But beneath the glittering exterior lies a nebula of self-centeredness, manipulation, and disregard for others.

These leaders have an uncanny knack for making every conversation about them. They expertly shift the focus of discussions to their achievements, experiences, and interests. You might find yourself wondering: how did a meeting about budget forecasts turn into a monologue about their golfing prowess?

A narcissistic leader might also be a maestro of manipulation. They may use tactics like gaslighting to make you question your reality or doubt your abilities. They are experts at exploiting others' vulnerabilities for their gain, making you feel valued one moment and utterly worthless the next.

Watch out for the blame game. When things go south, narcissistic leaders rarely take accountability. Instead, they are quick to point fingers, shirking responsibility and putting the burden on others. It's as if they believe their aura of 'perfection' makes them immune to mistakes.

One of the most striking traits of a narcissistic leader is their lack of empathy. It's not that they can't understand what you're feeling, but rather that they don't value it. Your emotions, challenges, or successes are often dismissed unless they serve their needs or agendas.

Let's not forget their sense of entitlement, which is as vast as the ocean. These leaders often believe they deserve more than others, whether it's respect, rewards, or recognition. They expect special treatment and get irritable or downright angry when they don't receive it.

Unravelling these behaviours is like decoding a complex puzzle. It's challenging but crucial for your well-being and growth. In the next section, we'll delve into strategies to navigate the turbulent waters of narcissistic leadership, keeping your confidence buoyant and your professional journey on course.

Remember, you're not just an extra in their show. You're the lead actor in your story. It's time to reclaim your spotlight.

Strategies for Navigating Narcissistic Leadership

Riding the Narcissistic Wave: Now that you're armed with an understanding of narcissism and its signs, let's equip you with the tools to ride this wave. This journey is about securing your peace, holding onto your confidence, and ensuring your professional progress doesn't capsize under a narcissistic leader.

1. Cultivate Emotional Intelligence:

Emotional intelligence is your armour on the battlefield of narcissistic leadership. This includes understanding your feelings, managing your reactions, and sailing through the treacherous seas of interpersonal relationships. Recognising your emotional triggers forms the keystone of this strategy.

For instance, if you realise your leader's constant criticism triggers feelings of inadequacy, use CBT self-soothing techniques like cognitive restructuring. This technique involves identifying and challenging negative thought patterns with positive, realistic ones. If you find yourself thinking, "I'm a failure," counteract it with, "Everyone makes mistakes. I can learn and improve." Another effective technique is mindfulness, where you focus on your present experiences in a non-judgmental manner, helping to alleviate stress and negative emotions.

2. Boundaries, Boundaries, Boundaries:

Remember this: No is a complete sentence. Establishing firm boundaries is a crucial step in protecting yourself. If your leader tries to pile on extra work beyond your scope, it's vital to communicate your limits.

Here's an empowering script you might use:

"I understand this task is important and am committed to delivering quality work. However, taking on additional projects would compromise the quality of my current workload. Can we discuss how to redistribute these tasks or reprioritise my workload?"

3. Document Everything:

In the world of a narcissistic leader, they're the hero, and everyone else is either a sidekick or a villain. Ensure your actions and words aren't twisted by keeping detailed records of your interactions, discussions, and achievements. Such records could prove to be invaluable during performance reviews, in disputing false allegations, or even in potential HR interventions.

4. Build a Support Network:

Creating allies within and outside the workplace can fortify your resilience. Your colleagues might be navigating similar waters. Support each other and share your experiences. Professional networks or mentors can provide fresh perspectives and valuable advice outside of work. You're part of a community, and there's strength in unity.

5. Strive for Self-care:

Your mental health is the compass guiding you through these stormy waters. Seeking a therapist can provide a safe harbour to unload your experiences and gain professional guidance. Engaging in relaxing activities such as yoga, meditation, or even a walk in the park can recharge your emotional batteries. Regular exercise, a balanced diet, and sufficient sleep can also enhance your mental resilience.

6. Plan Your Exit Strategy:

Despite your best efforts, if the work environment remains toxic, remember it's okay to abandon ship. Use the resources available— update your LinkedIn profile, polish your resume, and scan the horizon for new opportunities. Networking events and job platforms can provide a glimpse into other companies. You deserve a workspace where you're respected and valued.

Navigating the waves of narcissistic leadership isn't just about survival but about steering your professional journey towards growth. You're an extraordinary, robust, and resourceful professional. The storm of a leader's narcissism doesn't define your worth or forecast your potential. As the captain of your ship, embrace the waves, keep your sights on the horizon, and sail on.

Chapter 3

CAREER TRAUMA – UNDERSTANDING AND ACKNOWLEDGING ITS IMPACT

Let me speak from my heart: your struggle, your emotional pain and your enduring fight against the toxic, crippling effects of career trauma – they are all valid, and they deserve understanding and support. As an Executive Coach and Business Psychologist, I've been the confidante of countless individuals who have had their spirits marred by this scourge. Allow me to lead you deeper into the layers of this affliction.

The Unseen Scars of Career Trauma

Career trauma is an unseen yet potent wound. It manifests from repeated exposure to toxic workplace experiences. These can range from overt discrimination and abuse to the insidious drip-feed of microaggressions that slowly erode your self-esteem. And much like an untreated infection, career trauma quietly proliferates, spawning debilitating symptoms akin to those of Post-Traumatic Stress Disorder (PTSD), such as persistent anxiety, intrusive thoughts, flashbacks, or even nightmares.

The Silent Whispers of Career Trauma

This monster doesn't barge in with roars; it sneaks in on tiptoes, slowly numbing your sense of joy and achievement at work. The signs can be subtle: an unexplained anxiety that tightens your chest every Sunday night; a shroud of dread that hovers over your thoughts of work; a defensive stance in anticipation of the next attack; or a sudden hesitance to chase new opportunities, even when you're more than qualified.

A Glimpse into Career Trauma's Aftermath

Let me introduce you to Amina. A brilliant, driven woman, her presence used to light up any room until she crossed paths with a boss whose bigotry was as vast as his influence. Despite escaping to a healthier workplace, the ghost of her traumatic past looms large. The sight of anyone vaguely resembling her past tormentor sends her heart racing, her palms sweating, and her thoughts scattering—a classic trauma response. This perpetual state of alert, this continual expectation of threat, even in safe environments, is one of the lasting impacts of career trauma. It stifles potential, hinders progress, and casts long shadows on personal growth.

Healing from Career Trauma

Healing from career trauma is a journey that begins with acknowledging its existence and impact. The next critical step is seeking professional help—counsellors, therapists, or career coaches can provide invaluable support. However, don't discount the resources your current workplace might offer. Many organisations are waking up to the importance of mental health and have programs designed to provide support. Use them.

Asking for help, especially from HR, can feel uncomfortable. Here's a script to guide you:

"Could we discuss something that's been affecting my work performance? I'm dealing with residual effects from previous toxic work experiences and am interested in seeking professional help. Could you provide information on any mental health resources our company provides?"

Fortifying Your Resilience

Resilience is your armour in the battle against career trauma. Therapies like Cognitive Behavioural Therapy (CBT) can help you rewrite your trauma's narrative, helping you understand and change thought patterns that lead to harmful behaviours. Mindfulness and meditation techniques can also aid in maintaining composure during episodes of acute stress. Building a robust support network and prioritising self-care are other key elements of your healing journey.

Rising from the Ashes of Career Trauma

The path to recovery from career trauma is turbulent—it tests your resilience, your courage, and your endurance. However, remember, this trauma doesn't define you. It's merely a storm you're navigating. And like all storms, it will pass. Once it does, you'll emerge stronger, wiser, and ready to seize the opportunities that await you. On the other side of this trauma, there's a brighter, more inclusive world waiting for you.

Building Resilience – A Key to Overcoming Career Trauma

1. The Importance of Resilience in Professional Life

Resilience is a fundamental tool to help us bounce back from setbacks and adversity. In our professional lives, where challenges, failures, and disappointments are unavoidable, resilience allows us to weather these storms, learn from them, and bounce back stronger and wiser. The higher we climb the career ladder; the more resilience becomes a necessary attribute. It equips us with the mental strength to handle stress, overcome obstacles, deal with failure, and carry on, even when everything seems against us.

2. Techniques for Fostering Resilience

The beauty of resilience is that it can be cultivated and developed. Here are some practical techniques:

Gratitude Practice: Every day, take time to write down three things you're grateful for. They can be small wins or significant victories. This practice shifts your focus from what's going wrong to what's going right, fostering resilience by nurturing a positive mindset.

Affirmations: Affirmations are potent tools in reshaping our mental state. They are positive statements about the outcome you want to manifest. For instance, you can affirm, "I am a competent and successful professional. I handle challenges with wisdom and courage." Repeat these affirmations daily.

Mindfulness and meditation: These practices help you stay present and avoid getting caught up in negative thought cycles. They enable you to see challenges more objectively, reducing stress and promoting mental clarity.

Physical health: Exercise, adequate sleep, and a balanced diet contribute to resilience. They boost mood, improve cognitive function, and increase physical energy. This is one of my ways to stay resilient through the tough times that is so difficult to endure.

Your Faith: If you have a faith that you have leaned on for resilience but have stepped away because your confidence is low, consider reconnecting with it and the community your faith belongs to.

3. Resilience in Action

Amina is an ideal example of resilience in action. After experiencing career trauma, Amina felt her confidence and trust in the professional world was shattered. But she didn't remain in this state for long. She made a conscious choice to regain control over her career and mental health. She started incorporating resilience-building techniques into her daily routine.

She began a gratitude practice, listing down things she was thankful for daily, ranging from her supportive friends to her ability to make a difference in her job. Over time, she noticed her mindset shift from feeling victimised to feeling empowered.

Amina also used affirmations, consistently telling herself, "I am resilient. I can overcome any challenges that come my way." She noticed this started to shift her self-perception and reduce her anxiety.

Amina incorporated mindfulness and meditation into her routine, taking just 10 minutes a day to quiet her mind. This helped her reduce her stress levels and see her situation more clearly.

Finally, Amina paid attention to her physical health. She started regular exercise, made sure to get adequate sleep, and ate a balanced diet. This not only improved her mood and energy levels but also boosted her confidence.

Through these methods, Amina was able to overcome her career trauma and regain her confidence. She no longer feels trapped or helpless. Instead, she is in control, resilient, and ready to face any challenges that come her way.

Amina's story is a testament to the power of resilience. It proves that no matter how deep the wounds, we have the strength and the tools to heal, grow, and prosper.

Chapter 4

SELF-EMPOWERMENT –
THE FOUNDATION OF CONFIDENCE

Exploring the Concept of Self-empowerment

Self-empowerment is more than just a buzzword; it's a personal journey towards gaining control over one's own life, stepping into the driving seat, and taking the wheel. Self-empowerment is about acknowledging your inherent worth and capabilities and using that understanding as fuel to drive your life forward in the direction YOU want. This sense of personal power is not reliant on external validation or circumstances but is a wellspring from within that remains constant and intense, irrespective of life's ebb and flow.

Steps to Attain Self-Empowerment

The journey towards self-empowerment is personal and unique for everyone, yet there are common steps that are universally applicable:

- **Self-Understanding:** The first step to self-empowerment is understanding oneself. It involves acknowledging one's strengths, weaknesses, goals, and values. Self-understanding creates the foundation for personal growth and development.

- **Taking Responsibility:** We must take responsibility for our actions and decisions. Recognising that we are the architects of our lives empowers us to make positive changes.

- **Setting Goals and Making Plans:** Having a clear vision of where we want to go provides direction and purpose. Setting goals and making plans turns this vision into a roadmap towards self-empowerment.

- **Developing a Positive Mindset:** Maintaining a positive mindset, even in the face of adversity, can boost resilience and determination. Cultivating positive thinking practices such as gratitude and affirmations can be powerful tools in this process.

- **Intentionality:** Self-empowerment is not an incidental process; it requires deliberate intentionality. It's about committing to your personal growth and taking the reins of your development. Setting specific intentions anchors your actions in purpose, transforming your journey from a passive drift to a driven pursuit. With intention and action married together, the pathway to self-empowerment becomes not just a distant goal but a lived reality.

The Role of Self-empowerment in Building Confidence

Self-empowerment is the bedrock upon which confidence is built. When we empower ourselves, we gain a sense of control and mastery over our lives, which in turn enhances our confidence. As renowned life coach and author Anthony Robbins explains in his book 'Unlimited Power,' The pathway to personal power and achievement is understanding and applying the forces that shape human experience. Robbins asserts that by harnessing our inner resources, embracing self-empowerment, and instigating change from within, we can realise our full potential and cultivate the confidence needed to achieve our goals.

Confidence is not a static state; it's a dynamic process that evolves as we do. With each step of self-empowerment, we fortify our confidence, creating a positive feedback loop where increased self-empowerment boosts confidence, and enhanced confidence fuels further self-empowerment.

Oprah Winfrey, one of the most influential figures in media and arguably in the world, has frequently spoken about self-empowerment. Her powerful insights provide a fitting contribution to this chapter on self-empowerment.

"Think like a queen. A queen is not afraid to fail. Failure is another steppingstone to greatness," she once said. This resonates with the notion of self-empowerment, showing the importance of self-belief, courage, and resilience. Oprah encourages us to see failure not as an end but as an integral part of the journey towards self-empowerment and, ultimately, greatness.

Moreover, Oprah underscored the significance of taking charge of one's life by stating, "You don't become what you want. You become what you believe." This underlines the immense power of our beliefs in shaping our lives. If we believe in our worth and ability to achieve greatness, then that is the reality we will likely create.

This isn't to say that the journey to self-empowerment is easy. As Oprah says, "The thing you fear most has no power. Your fear of it is what has the power. Facing the truth really will set you free." This reminds us that self-empowerment often involves confronting and overcoming our fears.

The words of Oprah Winfrey remind us that self-empowerment is not merely about gaining strength or control. It's about recognising and embracing our intrinsic worth, overcoming our fears, and shaping our reality through our beliefs.

In conclusion, self-empowerment and confidence are intrinsically linked, fostering the other in a positive upward spiral. As you nurture your self-empowerment, you'll find your confidence growing in tandem, equipping you with the mental and emotional tools to navigate your professional journey, overcome career obstacles, and ascend to new heights of success.

Chapter 5

DEVELOPING A GROWTH MINDSET

A growth mindset is not just a buzzword thrown around in the professional field. It's a transformative concept that can make the difference between a plateauing career and an ever-evolving, dynamic one. In this chapter, we're diving deep into what a growth mindset is, its immense benefits for your career advancement, and how you can practically cultivate it.

Explanation of a Growth Mindset

A growth mindset is an attitude that thrives on challenges and sees failures not as evidence of unintelligence or incapacity but as a springboard for growth and stretching our abilities. It's about acknowledging our potential and understanding that our skills and abilities are not fixed but can be developed over time.

In her ground-breaking work, psychologist Carol Dweck found two broad categories of mindset: fixed and growth. Those with a fixed mindset tend to believe their capabilities are static and there's not much they can do to change them. They are often preoccupied with proving their intelligence or talent instead of developing them. Conversely, those with a growth mindset believe their abilities can be developed through dedication, hard work, and a love for learning.

The Benefits of a Growth Mindset for Career Advancement

For professionals, a growth mindset is a powerful tool in their arsenal. It fosters resilience in the face of setbacks and encourages continuous learning and skill development, which are crucial for advancement in today's fast-paced corporate world. With a growth mindset, feedback, even when critical, is viewed as a valuable resource for learning rather than a personal attack.

Moreover, a growth mindset pushes you out of your comfort zone, allowing you to take calculated risks. It fosters innovation, urges you to see beyond what's already established, and gives you the courage to navigate uncharted waters.

Consider the case of Thomas Edison, his invention of the light bulb didn't come easy—it came after 1,000 unsuccessful attempts. But did that deter him? No. Because he saw each failure as a stepping stone towards success, and that's the power of a growth mindset.

Practical Tips on Cultivating a Growth Mindset

Cultivating a growth mindset is not an overnight process; it's a continuous journey. Here are some practical steps to start:

1. **Embrace Challenges:** Start viewing challenges as opportunities to learn and grow rather than obstacles. When faced with a challenge, don't shy away—dive in!

2. **Learn from Criticism:** Constructive criticism is a great way to learn. Understand the intention behind the feedback and use it to improve.

3. **Celebrate Others' Success:** Instead of feeling threatened by others' success, learn from it. Celebrating others' achievements can motivate you to achieve your own.

4. **Value the Process Over the Outcome:** The focus should be on the journey of learning rather than the end result. Celebrate small wins and learn from failures.

5. **Replace 'I can't' with 'I can't yet':** This slight language change can make a significant impact on your mindset. It's not about whether you can do something but whether you can do it yet.

By practising these strategies, you are setting yourself up for an upward career trajectory fuelled by continuous growth and learning. A growth mindset is a key that unlocks potential, pushing you towards untapped territories in your professional journey.

While we've discussed the mechanics and benefits of a growth mindset, it's crucial to reinforce this point: a growth mindset is not limited by your background or race. This mentality is universal and transcends borders, cultures, and personal circumstances. It's the underpinning trait that most highly successful individuals across diverse fields share.

Consider some prominent personalities in history: Oprah Winfrey, Elon Musk, Barack Obama, and Maya Angelou. What do they have in common? Despite their vastly different backgrounds, each has exhibited a remarkable growth mindset. They continuously sought to learn and grow, overcoming immense challenges and adversity.

Oprah Winfrey, born into poverty and faced with numerous obstacles, became one of the most powerful women in media. Elon Musk, with no formal training in rocket science, leads one of the world's leading space exploration companies. Barack Obama, raised by a single mother and his grandparents, became the first African-American president of the United States. Having survived a childhood of trauma, Maya Angelou rose to become a revered poet and civil rights activist.

A growth mindset equips you with the tools to take the hardships and setbacks you've encountered and turn them into stepping stones. Regardless of your race or background, this mindset will propel you towards your personal and professional aspirations. No matter where you stand now, a growth mindset can unlock doors to opportunities and possibilities you may have never imagined.

So, as we conclude this chapter, I want you to reflect on your journey and start seeing your potential through a growth mindset lens. Adopting a growth mindset can be the turning point, no matter what hurdles you've encountered or how they've affected you. Let it be the wind beneath your wings, pushing you upward and onward. Be determined to grow and thrive, for that is the essence of a growth mindset."

Chapter 6

AMPLIFYING YOUR VOICE –
COMMUNICATION SKILLS FOR ADVOCACY

Effective communication is the bedrock of any thriving professional relationship. It can make or break your chances of professional advancement. However, effective communication isn't always easy, especially when your cultural background or personality type makes you naturally quieter or misunderstood. It is in these situations that one must learn to advocate for themselves while maintaining their authenticity.

The Importance of Effective Communication in the Workplace

Effective communication isn't just about expressing yourself clearly; it's also about understanding the perspectives of others. For some individuals, particularly introverts, the professional environment can seem overwhelming. They often have unique insights but struggle to communicate them due to their quieter disposition. On the other hand, extroverts, who are naturally vocal and expressive, can sometimes be misunderstood as being overbearing.

What's essential to remember is that the professional landscape is vast and varied. There's space for all communication styles to coexist and contribute to the vibrancy of the workplace. However, the challenge lies in cultivating a communication style that allows you to articulate your ideas while respecting your natural inclinations.

Tips for Effective Communication

Effective communication is a skill that can be honed with conscious effort and practice. Introverts may benefit from preparing and rehearsing key points in advance of meetings or presentations. This preparation can alleviate some of the anxiety associated with speaking up. For extroverts, practising active listening can ensure their enthusiasm doesn't overshadow others' voices.

In addition to practising these skills, understanding oneself is paramount in fostering effective communication. Personality assessments can provide valuable insights into your motivations, working styles, and communication preferences. One such assessment is the True Colors Personality Assessment.

True Colors Personality Assessment breaks down personality types into four colors: Gold, Green, Blue, and Orange. Each color represents a different set of characteristics.

- Gold personalities are dependable and organised and value rules and responsibilities.

- Green personalities are analytical, logical, and always on the lookout for learning opportunities and like their autonomy.

- Blue personalities are compassionate, empathetic, and cooperative, often bringing harmony to their groups.

- Orange personalities are spontaneous, energetic, and creative, bringing a sense of fun and excitement to their work.

Understanding your dominant color can help you leverage your strengths and address your challenges in communication. Moreover, by understanding the True Colors of others, you can tailor your communication style to better align with their preferences. This understanding creates a more inclusive and respectful communication environment.

Beyond this, cultivating emotional intelligence is also critical. Understanding your emotions and those of others can help you tailor your communication style to the situation. This is especially relevant when it comes to difficult conversations or moments of disagreement.

Chapter 7

HARNESSING THE POWER
OF NETWORKING AND MENTORSHIP

In the professional journey of many Black individuals, mentorship is a term that comes up time and again. Based on personal experience and observation, I believe that your manager should ideally be your mentor, provided they have done your job before. Continuously seeking numerous mentors can sometimes distract from the actual work, and while mentorship can be valuable, it should only be sought if there's a real need. More importantly, sponsorship is where our focus should lie.

The Role of Networking and Mentorship in Career Advancement

Effective networking and meaningful mentorship play a vital role in career advancement. Networking allows you to meet people who can provide support, knowledge, and opportunities. It builds a foundation for your career by creating solid relationships with people who can influence and facilitate your professional growth. Meanwhile, a mentor can guide you with their experience and wisdom. They can provide advice, feedback, and insight, helping you avoid costly mistakes and providing a roadmap to success.

Referencing Carla A Harris's book, *Strategize to Win*, she discusses a vital concept: Relationship Currency. This metaphorical currency is earned by investing in people and relationships. It's foundational in the professional world and can help open doors and secure opportunities.

Strategies for Effective Networking

Effective networking is an art that can be learned and honed over time. It involves more than just attending events and passing out business cards. It's about building and nurturing professional relationships that are mutual and beneficial. Remember, the aim is to establish authentic connections, not just a long list of contacts.

Here are some strategies:

1. **Be genuine and authentic**: People can sense insincerity. Be yourself and connect with others based on shared interests and values.

2. **Be helpful**: Networking is not just about taking. Offer help when you can, share information, and make introductions.

3. **Follow up**: Follow up with a simple email or message after meeting someone new. This keeps the connection alive and opens the door for future communication.

4. **Engage consistently**: Networking isn't a one-off event. Continuously engage with your network through social media, events, or casual catch-ups.

Finding and Benefiting from Mentors

A good mentor can provide valuable insights, advice, and encouragement. However, finding the right mentor is crucial. Look for someone who understands your industry and career path. They should also be someone who respects your individuality and is willing to invest their time and energy in your growth.

Remember, mentorship is a two-way street. Respect your mentor's time and show appreciation for their guidance. Apply the advice they give and update them on your progress.

Virtual Networking Strategies

The advent of Covid-19 has drastically changed the way we network. Physical events, conferences, and casual coffee meet-ups have given way to virtual meetings, webinars, and online networking events. However, we are starting to see more in-person events starting to take place again. This new virtual way presents new challenges but also new opportunities for building and maintaining a professional network.

1. **Adapt to the platform**: Different platforms have different norms and conventions. Make sure you're familiar with the platform's features and etiquette. For instance, using the chat function to engage in discussions or using virtual backgrounds to keep your space private can be helpful.

2. **Be visible**: Turn on your video whenever possible. This helps to create a more personal connection. Remember, your facial expressions and non-verbal cues are essential to your communication.

3. **Prepare your introduction**: With limited time and attention spans, having a concise and compelling introduction is key. An example could be, "Hi, I'm [Your Name], a [Your Job Title] at [Your Company]. I specialise in [Your Area of Specialization], and I'm currently focused on [Current Project or Goal]." This is a guideline so please make it your own.

4. **Engage with the content**: Whether it's a webinar, a meeting, or an online conference, engage with the content. Ask questions, provide insightful comments, and show your expertise.

5. **Follow-up promptly**: Virtual events can be overwhelming with information and new connections. Make sure to follow up with the people you've met promptly. A quick email or LinkedIn connection request can keep the conversation going.

6. **Keep nurturing the relationship**: Just like in-person networking, the relationship needs to be nurtured. Schedule regular catch-ups, share interesting articles or resources, and be supportive when they need it.

An example of an engaging opening statement for a virtual event:

"Hello, everyone, I'm [Your Name], and I work as [Your Job Title] at [Your Company]. I'm particularly passionate about [Your Area of Passion] and am currently exploring [Relevant Topic/Project/Goal]. I'd love to connect with like-minded professionals and learn from your experiences."

By adopting these strategies, you can make the most of virtual networking opportunities, expanding your reach and creating valuable connections without geographical limitations.

Example LinkedIn InMail to connect with a mentor outside of work:

Subject: Partnership Opportunity: Inviting You to Shape the Future of [Industry/Field]

Dear [Recipient's Name],

I hope this message finds you in the best of health and spirits. My name is [Your Name], and I am actively contributing to [Your Industry/Field] as a [Your Current Position]. Your profile captured my attention due to our shared passion for [Specific Area of Their Expertise], and I believe that together, we can drive even greater impact in our field.

In my quest to continually grow and innovate in [Your Industry/Field], I am seeking a mentorship partnership with a seasoned expert whose professional journey aligns with mine. Your extensive experience and accomplishments in [Their Industry/Field] resonate deeply with me, and I am confident that our collaboration could provide mutual value.

From this partnership, I anticipate engaging in rich dialogue about our industry, exchanging insights, and pushing the boundaries of our current understanding. I am eager to learn from your wisdom while bringing my perspective and unique approach to the table. My intention is to schedule brief, monthly check-ins that respect your time yet facilitate our collaboration.

I kindly invite you to consider my proposal and would be happy to share further information about my accomplishments, current projects, and future aspirations if you wish. I am thrilled about the possibility of working with a leader of your calibre and look forward to the opportunity to contribute to our shared industry.

Thank you for your time and consideration. I am optimistic about the potential impact of our collaboration and eagerly await your response.

Best regards,

[Your Name]

Chapter 8

POWERING YOUR CAREER WITH SPONSORSHIP

I often use the phrase: "Black people are over-mentored and under-sponsored." This powerful insight resonates deeply within the corridors of organisations. In the past, sponsorship has been a little-understood, exclusive aspect of corporate progression, an opportunity often limited to privileged circles. However, as organisations strive for diversity and inclusion, sponsorship is now taking a formalised shape and is key to promoting a sustainable, diverse workforce. If leveraged correctly, it has the power to break glass ceilings, offering Black professionals a catapult to leadership roles and expansive opportunities.

The significance of sponsorship in career advancement

A Centre for Talent Innovation study found that professionals of color are 44% less likely than their white counterparts to have a sponsor. This is not due to overlooking the potential of sponsorship but a lack of awareness about its transformative influence. When a well-respected figure within your organisation becomes your champion, promoting your skills, talents, and potential to others in influential positions, your career can take a rapid upward trajectory.

Differentiating between a mentor and a sponsor

It's vital to understand that a mentor is not a sponsor. A mentor provides guidance, while a sponsor advocates for you, opening doors and endorsing you for opportunities that could be otherwise inaccessible. They navigate the influential spheres of your organisation on your behalf, speaking for you in rooms you're not in, creating that pivotal visibility.

Strategies for securing a sponsor

Unlike securing a mentor, acquiring a sponsor requires showcasing your value and potential to the organisation. It's about laying out your contributions and demonstrating your commitment to growth. Start by identifying influential individuals within the organisation who could act as sponsors. Then, invest time in strategic stakeholder mapping, which helps identify key individuals and build beneficial relationships.

Tips on how to maintain and nurture sponsor relationships

Maintaining a sponsor relationship demands a proactive approach. Regularly share your progress and achievements while also showing interest in their work. Be receptive to feedback, showing your eagerness to learn and grow. Always remember that this should be a mutually beneficial relationship.

The role of formal sponsorship
programs in organisations and how to leverage them

Many organisations now offer formal sponsorship programs, a significant step towards breaking down barriers and promoting diversity. If such a program exists within your organisation, I encourage you to utilise it fully. If not, it might be time to push for its creation, underlining the value such initiatives bring to an organisation's diversity and growth.

Securing a sponsor is not just about advancing within your current organisation but about career sustainability, strategic positioning, and meaningful contribution. Sponsorship can be an immense game-changer in your career's narrative.

My question is, are you ready to redefine your career trajectory? Are you prepared to secure a sponsor and unlock doors you might not have even known existed? Remember, the future is in your hands.

Here are 2 examples of how to approach potential sponsors via email:

Example 1:

Subject: Introduction and Inquiry about Sponsorship Opportunities

Dear [Potential Sponsor's Name],

I hope this email finds you well. My name is [Your Name], and I am currently working as a [Your Position] in the [Your Department] of our organisation. Over the years, I have admired your leadership style and the contributions you have made to [Company's Name]. Your work, particularly in [mention specific project or role they had], has left a significant impact and is something I deeply resonate with.

Recently, I've been seeking opportunities to develop my skills further, learn from experienced leaders, and make meaningful contributions to the company. In my research, I came across the idea of Sponsorship. Having a sponsor within our organisation would provide invaluable support and guidance as I strive to make more significant contributions and grow in my role.

I admire your work and align with your vision for our company, and I believe there could be potential for you to act as my sponsor. I'd love to share more about my experience, my contributions to the company so far, and my future goals over a coffee or a brief meeting at a time that suits you.

Would you be available sometime next week to discuss this further?

Thank you for considering my request. I look forward to potentially working more closely with you.

Best regards,

[Your Name]

Example 2:

Subject: Exploring the Possibility of Sponsorship

Hello [Potential Sponsor's Name],

I hope this message finds you well. My name is [Your Name], and I am currently serving in the role of [Your Position] within the [Your Department]. Over the past [number of years/months in the position], I have dedicated myself to [briefly describe a significant contribution or project].

Your impact within [Company's Name] is one that I deeply respect and admire. Your leadership and strategic guidance in [mention specific project or role they had] have truly transformed our organisation and inspired my own ambitions.

As I strive to enhance my role and make a more substantial impact within our company, I understand the value of sponsorship in career progression. Unlike mentorship, sponsorship offers more influential support through advocacy and strategic guidance.

Considering this, I'm contacting you because your sponsorship could greatly aid my professional growth and amplify my contributions to our shared goals at [Company's Name]. Given your impactful role and my aspirations aligning with your area of expertise, I'd be interested in discussing the potential for you to act as my sponsor.

Would you be open to a meeting at a convenient time over the next week? I'd be eager to share more about my aspirations, my current contributions to the company, and how I envision this sponsorship could be mutually beneficial.

Thank you for considering my proposal. I look forward to further discussing this and potentially benefiting from your influential support within the company.

Sincerely,

[Your Name]

LinkedIn InMail Example for Sponsorship:

Here is an example of how you could approach someone on LinkedIn for sponsorship. Feel free to copy and paste and make changes as you see fit.

Subject: Seeking Sponsorship for Professional Growth

Hello [Potential Sponsor's Name],

I hope this message finds you well. Allow me to introduce myself; my name is [Your Name], and I'm currently [Your Position] at [Your Company]. I've been following your work in [mention their field or company] and have been deeply inspired by your impactful contributions and leadership.

I'm writing this message today because I'm seeking to elevate my professional journey and make significant contributions in my own right within our industry. In my research and experience, I've found that one of the most effective catalysts for such progress is not just mentorship but sponsorship.

Sponsorship, with its emphasis on advocacy and strategic guidance, seems an invaluable asset in achieving my career objectives. I firmly believe that a sponsor with your experience and insights could provide me with a unique and valuable perspective that I may not have access to within my current organisation.

I am eager to explore the possibility of you becoming my sponsor. While I am fully aware of the time and commitment sponsorship can entail, I am confident that my dedication, willingness to learn, and commitment to our industry could mutually benefit this relationship.

Would you be open to a brief virtual meeting at a time that suits you to discuss this potential? I would appreciate the opportunity to share my aspirations, the steps I am taking towards these goals, and how I envision your sponsorship could further enhance my contribution to our industry.

I understand that you are extremely busy, and I appreciate your consideration. I look forward to the possibility of collaborating with you to make a significant impact in our industry.

Sincerely,

[Your Name]

Chapter 9

HARNESSING THE POWER OF THE RETICULAR ACTIVATING SYSTEM (RAS) TO REBUILD CONFIDENCE

Have you ever heard of the Reticular Activating System? If not, then check it out.

The Reticular Activating System (RAS) is a network of neurons in the brainstem that serves as a gatekeeper for information that travels to your conscious mind. The RAS plays a crucial role in attention and focus, ultimately deciding what gets noticed and what goes unnoticed.

Understanding and leveraging the RAS can be a game-changer in the realm of confidence and personal growth. It can help us redirect our focus towards our strengths, potential, positive outcomes and away from self-doubt and negativity.

Understanding the Reticular Activating System

The RAS acts as a filter for the constant influx of information we encounter daily, allowing only certain information to pass to our conscious minds. Dr Sarah McKay, neuroscientist and author of "The Women's Brain Book", points out, "The RAS acts as a gatekeeper, allowing in only information that is important enough to gain our conscious attention."

This filtration process is based on our beliefs, values, and focus. For example, when you buy a new car, suddenly you start seeing the same model everywhere. That's your RAS in action, prioritising information that is currently important or relevant to you.

The RAS and Confidence Building

How does the RAS relate to building confidence? Our beliefs and self-perceptions heavily influence the information our RAS lets through. If you hold negative beliefs about your abilities or consistently focus on your shortcomings, your RAS will filter in evidence supporting these beliefs, further undermining your confidence.

On the other hand, by consciously shifting our focus and beliefs towards positivity and our inherent strengths, the RAS will start filtering in affirming information. Over time, this strengthens our confidence and self-belief as we begin noticing more instances of our capabilities and successes.

Strategies for Leveraging the RAS

Here are some practical steps to harness your RAS for confidence building:

1. **Positive Affirmations**: Affirmations are positive statements that can help you to challenge and overcome self-sabotaging and negative thoughts. They are typically in the present tense and are personal in nature. For example, if you struggle with confidence in your professional abilities, your affirmation could be, "I am skilled, experienced, and capable in my job." The key to effective affirmations is repetition. Write them down, say them out loud, and put them on post-it notes around your workspace or home. The more frequently you see and recite your affirmations, the stronger the message to your RAS that this is essential information.

2. **Visualization** involves creating a vivid mental picture of your desired outcome or goal. It's more than just daydreaming - it requires focused intent. For instance, if you want to become a confident public speaker, visualise yourself standing on a stage, delivering your speech clearly, confidently, and with great

applause. Picture the audience's positive reactions, your sense of accomplishment and pride. Visualisation convinces your RAS that this is your reality, making it prioritise information and opportunities that will help you achieve this.

3. **Mindfulness and Focus**: Mindfulness involves being fully engaged in the present moment without judgment. It helps you become more aware of your thoughts and feelings, which can be a powerful tool in directing your focus. If you find your thoughts drifting towards self-doubt or criticism during a project, you can use mindfulness to gently guide your focus back to your capabilities and the task at hand. A simple way to practice mindfulness is through focused breathing exercises, even for a few minutes daily.

4. **Personal Development**: Push yourself out of your comfort zone and take on new challenges that can help you grow. This could be learning a new skill, taking on a challenging project, or seeking additional responsibilities. For instance, if you're nervous about leading team meetings, volunteer to do it. As you successfully navigate these experiences, they provide concrete evidence to your RAS of your capabilities. Celebrate these victories, no matter how small, as they all contribute to reinforcing your self-confidence.

By consistently implementing these strategies, you will begin to see a shift in your focus, beliefs, and, ultimately, your self-confidence. The goal is to train your Reticular Activating System to consistently filter in positivity and successes; over time, these will become your new norm.

Chapter 10

CHARTING YOUR PATH FORWARD

Congratulations on reaching this transformative juncture in your career journey. You've absorbed knowledge, insights, and strategies throughout this book, and now it's time to channel that newfound wisdom into decisive action. Remember, your journey is uniquely yours, and your confidence is a formidable force propelling you forward. Harness it, take the reins, and chart your path with unyielding determination.

Creating a Personal Roadmap for Career Progression

A personal roadmap is not just a career plan. It's an empowering tool that provides clarity, direction, and a deep understanding of where you're going, why you're going there, and what steps you'll take to get there.

Start by reflecting on what you've learned about yourself throughout this journey. What are your strengths, your passions, and your values? What challenges do you face, and what resources do you have at your disposal? Then, envision your desired destination, that pinnacle of professional success. It's essential to be specific here: What does it look like? What does it feel like?

Armed with this self-awareness and clarity, create a roadmap that aligns your career goals with your authentic self. Include short-term milestones and long-term objectives and chart the steps you'll take to achieve them. Remember to consider potential roadblocks and devise contingency plans to overcome them.

Setting Achievable Career Goals

Goal setting is a vital step in your journey. SMART goals (Specific, Measurable, Achievable, Relevant, and Time-bound) can guide you on your path, ensuring each step you take brings you closer to your destination.

Consider the sponsorship and mentorship opportunities you've explored in previous chapters when setting your goals. Consider your growth mindset, your confidence, resilience, and self-empowerment. How can you weave these into your goals? Goals should drive not only your career advancement but also your personal growth.

Maintaining Momentum and Continuing Professional Growth

Maintaining momentum is where many of us falter. It's one thing to start strong and quite another to sustain that strength throughout the journey. This is where consistency and resilience play vital roles.

One strategy is to build a habit of lifelong learning. This could mean subscribing to industry publications, attending webinars, or enrolling in online courses. Another strategy is to join a professional organisation in your field, which can provide networking opportunities, professional development resources, and a community of like-minded professionals.

As you know, I'm passionate about sharing career advice. Subscribing to my podcast and watching my YouTube channel can be part of your daily self-development ritual. I regularly cover topics such as overcoming career trauma, building resilience, developing a growth mindset, and more.

The Power of Taking Action

Lastly, remember that the journey towards success starts with taking action. Commit to your goals, commit to your growth, and commit to your success. Understand that this is a journey you alone must undertake - it's yours to shape, with your newfound confidence as your compass.

As we've discovered, confidence is key to charting your path forward. Believe in your abilities, believe in your worth, and believe in your potential to shape your professional destiny. It's not about leaving your career progression to chance; it's about taking charge, confidently navigating your course, and steering your career towards success.

To borrow words from the phenomenal Maya Angelou, "Success is liking yourself, liking what you do, and liking how you do it." So, chart your path, take that leap, and redefine success on your own terms. Remember, there's nothing you cannot achieve. The power is in your hands.

You're now on the precipice of a remarkable journey brimming with learning, growth, and potential. It's time to take that step forward, to confidently flip the page and commence a new chapter. You're ready. The world is ready for you. Now, let's make it happen.

Chapter 11

THE POWER OF GRATITUDE: CULTIVATING CONFIDENCE AND POSITIVITY

Gratitude is a transformative practice that profoundly influences our mental and emotional state and, by extension, our confidence. By focusing our attention on things, we appreciate, we shift our mindset from one of scarcity to one of abundance. This shift serves to strengthen our self-belief, resilience, and overall well-being, bolstering our confidence.

The concept of gratitude is not new. Philosophers and spiritual teachers have long espoused the virtues of thankfulness. Recent research in positive psychology has provided empirical support to these age-old pearls of wisdom, demonstrating a robust association between gratitude and greater happiness.

Practising Gratitude

One of the most effective ways to cultivate gratitude is by maintaining a gratitude journal. Writing our blessings magnifies our positive feelings and helps us relish good experiences. It pushes negativity to the periphery, reducing stress and fostering a sense of calm and contentment.

Make it a daily or weekly practice to jot down things you're grateful for. It could be something as simple as a good cup of coffee or as grand as a promotion at work. Over time, you will see your perspective broadening, your spirits lifting, and your confidence growing.

Personal Example of Gratitude Practice

In my personal experience, I've found connecting with a gratitude buddy to be an enriching practice. My friend Linda and I share our daily gratitude via voice notes on WhatsApp. This ritual serves as a moment of pause, a celebration of the day's blessings, no matter how small. It's incredibly uplifting and a mood booster, especially when we anticipate a particularly challenging day. The routine reinforces positivity, ultimately strengthening our confidence and resilience.

More Ways to Cultivate Gratitude

Beyond journaling and gratitude buddies, there are other ways to foster gratitude. You can practice mindfulness, where you take a few minutes each day to savour the moment and the environment around you. Expressing thanks to those around you for their kindness and support also helps to nurture gratitude. This could be in the form of a handwritten note, a small gift, or even just a sincere verbal acknowledgement.

Gratitude and Confidence

So, how does gratitude contribute to building confidence? Focusing on positive aspects of your life and acknowledging your successes, however small, reinforces self-belief. Over time, as you observe the good in your life, you also begin to recognise your worth and capabilities, strengthening your confidence.

Moreover, gratitude fosters resilience. When faced with challenges, looking back at your gratitude journal or remembering your shared expressions of thanks helps to put things in perspective. It reminds you of your past successes, of the love and support you have, and of your personal strength. This, in turn, bolsters your confidence to face whatever comes your way.

In conclusion, integrating gratitude into your daily routine can significantly enhance your confidence and overall sense of well-being. It offers a positive lens through which to view the world, fostering resilience and a sense of contentment. It's a simple yet powerful practice that yields far-reaching benefits and one I highly recommend.

Chapter 12

THE TRANSFORMATIVE POWER OF VISIONING

Visioning is not just another buzzword; it's a transformative practice that's reshaped my life and has the potential to redefine yours. As a Business Coach Psychologist, I've seen first-hand how visioning can move you from a state of confusion to one of empowered clarity. In this chapter, we'll delve into the psychological underpinnings of visioning, the pioneers who brought it to prominence, and the step-by-step process that can bring your grandest aspirations to life. So, are you ready to cast your vision?

The Psychology of Visioning

At its core, visioning taps into multiple areas of psychology including Positive Psychology, Cognitive Behavioural Therapy (CBT), and Emotional Intelligence. Visioning essentially asks you to entertain the "What if?" question constructively, encouraging a shift from a fixed to a growth mindset.

Dr. Barbara Fredrickson, a renowned psychologist, introduced the 'Broaden-and-Build' theory, suggesting that positive emotions broaden your sense of possibilities and open your mind, enabling you to build new skills and resources. This aligns perfectly with visioning, which first asks you to envision a future filled with accomplishments and joy and then guides you to build the path towards it.

The Father of Visioning: Ron Lippitt

The term "visioning" was notably coined by organizational psychologist Ron Lippitt in the context of community planning and organizational development. Lippitt emphasized the importance of a shared vision as a critical element for effective leadership and change. His work laid the foundations that allowed visioning to evolve into the transformative personal development tool it is today.

My Journey with Visioning

Before I became a Business Coach Psychologist, I, too, was on a journey of self-discovery and growth. Visioning played a pivotal role. Unlike simple goal-setting, visioning allowed me to attach emotions to my goals. Each vision was not just a statement but a vivid, multi-sensory experience. Whenever setbacks occurred—and believe me, they did—the emotional richness of my vision served as a lighthouse, guiding me back to my path.

Step-By-Step to Your Vision

Set the Stage: Find a quiet, comfortable place where you won't be disturbed. This is your sacred space for visioning. Sit or lie down and take deep, calming breaths.

Mindfulness: Engage in a few minutes of mindfulness or meditation to clear your mind. Let go of all distractions and focus on your breathing.

Emotional Priming: Think about moments when you've felt incredibly proud, fulfilled, or happy. Relive them in your mind to emotionally prime yourself.

Start Visioning: Let your imagination go wild. What does your ideal life look like 5 or 10 years from now? Visualize it in as much detail as possible. Where are you? Who are you with? What are you doing?

Engage the Senses: Make your vision multi-sensory. What can you hear, smell, taste, or touch in your ideal future?

Attach Emotion: This is where the magic happens. Attach deep, strong emotions to your vision. How does achieving this vision make you feel?

Affirm and Manifest: Conclude your visioning session by affirming your vision. Turn it into a statement or mantra that you can repeat daily.

Document: Write down what you've envisioned. This makes it tangible and serves as a reference.

Create a Vision Board: If you're a visual person, supplement your written vision with images and quotes that resonate with your future state.

Review and Adapt: Periodically revisit your vision, especially when you feel lost or encounter setbacks. It will serve as your North Star.

The Versatility of Visioning: Real-World Scenarios

Visioning is not a one-size-fits-all concept; its applications are as diverse as your aspirations. Here, we'll explore various scenarios where visioning can make a dramatic difference in the outcomes you seek.

Short-Term Visioning

While visioning is often associated with long-term goals, it's equally powerful for short-term objectives. If you're preparing for a public speaking event next month, for instance, envision yourself commanding the room with poise and confidence. Feel the applause, hear the laughter at your well-timed jokes, and sense the admiration from your audience. You don't always have to cast your vision years into the future; sometimes, a few weeks or months ahead is all you need to supercharge your actions.

Visioning for Job Hunting: A Case Study

One of my clients found herself at a crossroads; she was eager to switch jobs and stumbled upon a role that seemed tailor-made for her skill set. I suggested that she print off the job description and start envisioning her "perfect fit" role. She envisioned the joy she'd feel waking up for work, the dynamic interactions with colleagues, the sense of accomplishment at the end of each day, and even the clothes that would make her feel most confident.

When she stepped into interviews for that role, she was already emotionally connected to it. She could articulate not just why she was a good fit, but also how much the role aligned with her career vision. Needless to say, she nailed the interviews and got the job.

Scripting and Visioning: A Dynamic Duo

If you're someone who loves to write, visioning pairs marvellously with scripting. Scripting allows you to put your vision into words, detailing the events as if they have already occurred. This practice adds another layer of tangibility to your vision. After a visioning session, jot down the events and feelings you experienced. Revisit this script regularly to further cement your vision.

Visioning for Interview Prep: Level Up Your Confidence

Knowing who will interview you can be a game-changer, thanks to visioning. My recommendation is to look them up on LinkedIn, get a sense of their professional background and demeanour, and then incorporate this information into your visioning practice. Imagine the interview going splendidly, with a natural flow of conversation, and mutual respect evident in every interaction.

By the time you sit in the actual interview, your visioning exercise will have given you a "rehearsed spontaneity." You'll feel less like you're venturing into unknown territory and more like you're stepping into a scene you've already successfully lived. This takes your confidence to a whole new level, setting you up for interview success.

Quick Tips for Visioning in Varied Scenarios

Career Progression: If you're looking to climb the corporate ladder, envision yourself in that corner office, leading high-stakes meetings, or being the keynote speaker at an industry event.

Work-Life Balance: For those re-entering the workforce, especially after parental leave, envision a balanced life where you excel both at home and work. Feel the fulfilment and the balance.

Fitness Goals: Imagine yourself crossing the finish line of a marathon, or achieving that tricky yoga pose you've been working on. Feel the sweat, the exhaustion, and the immense pride.

Building Confidence: Envision scenarios where you assert yourself clearly and confidently. Whether it's negotiating a pay raise or standing up for what you believe in, see yourself doing it, and feel the subsequent boost in self-esteem.

Networking: If you're attending an industry event or conference, envision meaningful connections and enlightening conversations. Imagine yourself exchanging business cards with key influencers in your field.

The Challenges of Visioning and How to Overcome Them

Not everyone finds visioning to be second nature. People differ in their ability to form mental images or attach emotions to their thoughts. This can be due to various factors, from scepticism about the efficacy of visioning to a simple lack of practice in using one's imagination in this particular way.

Taking Baby Steps: The Gradual Approach

If you find visioning challenging, that's okay! Here's a gentle approach to ease you into the practice:

Start Small: Dedicate just a few minutes each day to visioning. You don't have to see your entire life plan; maybe just envision the upcoming weekend.

Go Visual First: Initially, focus on visual elements. See yourself accomplishing a small goal, like completing a project or having a successful meeting. Don't worry if the images aren't vivid initially; it's the repetition that counts.

Add the Emotional Layer: Once you're comfortable with the visual aspect, begin to tap into the feeling part. Imagine the sense of achievement, the joy, or even the relief you'd feel.

Note Your Observations: As you visualize, you might start to see specific faces or places. Recognize what comes up; these could be hints from your subconscious about what truly matters to you.

Feel the Sensations: You might begin to notice physical sensations, like a tingling in your hands or a warmth in your stomach. These are good indicators that you're emotionally connected to your vision.

Track Progress: Keep a visioning journal. Write down what you saw, felt, and any physical sensations you experienced.

Consistency is Key: The 21-Day Rule

You might have heard the adage that it takes 21 days to form a habit. While this is a general guideline and can vary from person to person, it does underscore the importance of consistency. The more you practice, the more natural visioning will feel, and the more impactful it will become in your life.

The Empowering Impact of Daily Visioning

Daily application of visioning can lead to profound changes. You'll not only become better at envisioning more vivid and emotive scenes, but you'll also start seeing positive shifts in your daily life. As someone who has extensively used visioning in my own career journey and has successfully coached others in applying it, I can vouch for its transformative power. And hey, if you're aiming to rock that job interview or nail that project presentation, wouldn't you want every tool at your disposal? Make visioning one of those go-to tools!

CONCLUSION

Your Transformative Journey Starts Now

Congratulations, you've made it to the end of this life-changing journey! But let's be clear: reaching this point is not the end; it's just the beginning of a new, empowered chapter in your life. So, pause for a moment. Reflect on the treasure trove of knowledge, strategies, and wisdom you've just encountered.

One Action, Infinite Possibilities

Ask yourself: "What is one action from this book that I can start implementing today?" Got it? Good! Now think about how making that change would affect you if you were more confident. Picture the radiant smiles, the approving nods, the open doors—both professionally and personally.

The 21-Day Challenge

Write down the action you've chosen and make it a point to practice it consistently for the next 21 days. Remember, it takes about 21 days to form a new habit. Let's make this new version of you a habit! And let's not keep the excitement to ourselves; stay connected by following my YouTube channel where we'll dive even deeper into these transformative tools.

Impact and Beyond

Your well-being and relationships stand to benefit immensely from this newfound confidence. Imagine sitting down to dinner with your loved ones, walking into a business meeting, or even simply looking at yourself in the mirror with an air of certainty that wasn't there before. That's the impact we're talking about!

Share the Wealth

If this book has made even a fraction of an impact on your life, why not amplify that effect by sharing it with someone else? Send them a link, take a celebratory selfie with the book, or better yet, gift them a copy. Let's spread the ripple of transformation far and wide.

Time to Soar

So what are you waiting for? The world is not just a stage; it's an arena, and it's waiting for you to conquer it. Stride forward, head held high, armed with the tools, strategies, and most importantly, the mindset that will help you claim your space in it. Your future self will thank you, I guarantee it.

And if you ever find yourself faltering, always remember: You've got this, and I've got your back. Here's to your journey toward unstoppable confidence and limitless potential!

Believe in yourself, embrace your journey, and unleash your brilliance.

And please subscribe to my YouTube Channel for helpful content.

Xoxo, KK Harris

Please follow me on my social media which includes my YouTube channel,
Instagram and a link to this book.

When you follow let me know that you bought the book so
I can personally thank you.

Kind regards,

KK Harris